Limitless
Defy the Ordinary

STUDY GUIDE

Copyright © 2021 by Eric Petree

Published by AVAIL

All rights reserved. No portion of this book may be reproduced, stored in a retrieval system, or transmitted in any form or by any means—electronic, mechanical, photocopy, recording, scanning, or other—except for brief quotations in critical reviews or articles, without prior written permission of the author.

Scripture quotations marked KJV are taken from the King James Version of the Bible. Public domain. Scripture quotations marked NIV are taken from the Holy Bible, New International Version®, NIV®. Copyright © 1973, 1978, 1984, 2011 by Biblica, Inc.™ Used by permission of Zondervan. All rights reserved worldwide. www.zondervan.com. The "NIV" and "New International Version" are trademarks registered in the United States Patent and Trademark Office by Biblica, Inc.™ | Scripture quotations marked ESV are taken from the Holy Bible, English Standard Version, Copyright © 2001 by Crossway, a publishing ministry of Good News Publishers. Used by permission. All rights reserved.

For foreign and subsidiary rights, contact the author.

Cover design: Joe DeLeon
Cover photo: Adrian Payne Photography

ISBN: 978-1-954089-10-5   1 2 3 4 5 6 7 8 9 10

Printed in the United States of America

Defy the Ordinary

ERIC PETREE

STUDY GUIDE

AVAIL

CONTENTS

Chapter 1. Introduction 6

Chapter 2. Go Fly A Kite 12

Chapter 3. Here to There 20

Chapter 4. See 'N Say 30

Chapter 5. Flux Capacity 38

Chapter 6. Defining Moments 46

Chapter 7. Within Reach 54

Chapter 8. Tuned by Tension 64

Chapter 9. A Room With a View 72

Chapter 10. A Blessing Called Rejection 80

Chapter 11. The Seventh Wave 90

Chapter 12. That's Life 98

Chapter 13. Finding Your Greatness 108

Introduction

As long as we walk on this fallen earth, we will encounter impossible situations and treacherous boundaries. Yet for those who know and love God, let us walk with our head high and heart pointed toward heaven, each foot a step closer to the limitless life our limitless God has created for you and me, right here and right now.

REVIEW

Read the Introduction in Limitless: Defy the Ordinary, *reflect on the text, and answer the questions below.*

When you think of the characteristics of God, do you count "limitless" among them? What does that mean to you?

_____
_____
_____
_____
_____
_____
_____
_____
_____

Do you perceive your life as one of abundance or restriction? Explain your choice.

_____
_____
_____
_____
_____
_____
_____
_____

REFLECT

Now to him who is able to do far more abundantly than all that we ask or think, according to the power at work within us ...
(Ephesians 3:20, ESV)

Reflect on the passage above and answer the following question:

Do you live a life that reflects His limitless nature?

_____
_____
_____
_____
_____
_____
_____
_____
_____
_____

RESPOND

Do you feel like you are thriving in life or merely surviving? What does thriving look like to you?

_____
_____
_____
_____
_____
_____
_____
_____
_____
_____

What changes do you need to make that will usher the abundance of God into your mind and heart? Are you ready to make them?

_____
_____
_____
_____
_____
_____
_____
_____
_____
_____
_____

chapter 1

Go Fly A Kite

No matter how persuasive you are in convincing yourself your dreams are impossible or nonexistent, the truth is that God has given you a dream—a limitless one that can't be contained within walls or below a ceiling. He has equipped you with the desire and the tools necessary to fulfill His dream for your life. It's time to take the limits off your dream.

REVIEW

Read Chapter 1: "Go Fly A Kite" in Limitless: Defy the Ordinary, *reflect on the text, and answer the questions below.*

In the book of Proverbs, Solomon writes that without vision, the people will perish. This particular translation of vision is "dream." Why do you think the absence of a dream would lead to such dire consequences?

_____
_____
_____
_____
_____
_____
_____
_____

What dreams did you have when you were young? Do you feel like you have lived those? If not, when and why did you push those dreams aside?

_____
_____
_____
_____
_____
_____
_____

Kite-flying is an apt metaphor for generating and following through on your dreams and vision, given that the necessary steps to launch the kite are similar to the ones you need to launch your dreams. Consider your own dreams and how they might be realized by employing the following methods.

A kite requires resistance to keep it in the air. It only works when it is flying against the wind. When you encounter resistance, do you allow it to shut you down, or do you know how to use it to your advantage?

_____
_____
_____
_____
_____

When it comes to most endeavors, including kite-flying, two are better than one. The company you keep will have a significant impact on your vision and its trajectory. Do the people in your life enable or inhibit the pursuit of your dreams and the fulfillment of your calling? Are there certain relationships you need to reevaluate?

_____
_____
_____
_____
_____

It is critically important to take stock and be aware of your environment. If you're flying a kite, oblivious to the condition of the ground below or the trees above, you've got a great shot of twisting an ankle or landing your kite in a tree. The same goes for your life. Are you aware of the potential obstacles and pitfalls before you? What is your plan to navigate the difficult paths that lie between you and your dreams?

_____

_____

_____

_____

_____

Consider the necessity of the professional kite flyer to adapt to changing conditions on the fly. How do you respond to change? Are you able to adapt, or do you find yourself paralyzed when your circumstances shift? What are ways you can become more adaptable to changes you encounter?

_____

_____

_____

_____

_____

REFLECT

"Write the vision; make it plain on tablets, so he may run who reads it" (Habakkuk 2:2, ESV).

Reflect on the passage above and answer the following questions:

In Habakkuk 2, we observe God speaking to Habakkuk, instructing him to write his vision down. In so doing, Habakkuk would not only be fortifying his own faith but that of others. Why do you think it was imperative for Habakkuk to have and articulate his vision?

_____
_____
_____
_____
_____
_____

Do you believe God has instilled a vision for your life within you? If so, do you know what it is? If not, do you think there is a reason your life (or your perception of it) lacks vision?

_____
_____
_____
_____
_____
_____
_____

Do you feel like you have a firm grip on your dreams, or have they slipped through your fingers? Do you trust that God desires your vision and can reconnect you with it?

_____
_____
_____
_____
_____
_____
_____

RESPOND

When there is no wind to lift your kite into the air, you have to run and create your own. What are the winds like in your life right now? Do you need to start running? What are ways you can generate forward momentum?

_____
_____
_____
_____
_____

What baggage are you holding on to that is preventing you from moving forward? How can you begin to lay those burdens down?

_____
_____
_____
_____
_____

If your dream is within sight, what is holding you back from letting it soar?

_____
_____
_____
_____
_____

chapter 2

Here to There

What you see "there" will determine whether or not you leave "here." You have to know where you're going, or you'll never go anywhere.

REVIEW

Read Chapter 2: "Here to There" in Limitless: Defy the Ordinary, *reflect on the text, and answer the questions below.*

Brandon reached a make-or-break point in his life. In what ways do you identify with him? Can you remember a turning point in your life? Have you turned? If not, what's holding you back?

_____
_____
_____
_____
_____
_____
_____

Can you answer the following question: If you had unlimited funds, unlimited resources, and all the time in the world, what would you do? If so, write your answer below. If not, can you identify what's blocking you from verbalizing your dream?

_____
_____
_____
_____
_____
_____
_____
_____
_____

If you are to reach your intended destination and expect any amount of longevity, you have to put in the work. Shortcuts and loopholes leave you unprepared to live out your dreams.

Why do you think that is, and are you aware of shortcuts you have taken that caused more harm than good?

_____
_____
_____
_____
_____
_____
_____
_____
_____

New beginnings and endeavors are typically exciting, buoyed by beginning momentum. However, fatigue, distraction, or boredom can sap your energy and stall your dreams even over a short time. Have you experienced this before? Are you experiencing it now? If so, how motivated are you to rediscover your momentum?

_____
_____
_____
_____
_____

The space program represents some of the best of human achievement. When you compare the Apollo 11 moon landing and the Apollo 13 near-tragedy, can you identify success within both? How does it differ from one to another?

_____
_____
_____
_____
_____

Your current present was once your past future, but now, you are "here." So, what's next? Do you have a "there"?

_____
_____
_____
_____
_____

What challenges or obstacles exist between where you are currently and where you want to go?

_____
_____
_____
_____
_____
_____
_____

How do you interpret the differences between success and significance? What role do others play in your journey from "here" to "there"?

_____
_____
_____
_____
_____
_____
_____

REFLECT

Where there is no vision, the people will perish (Proverbs 29:18a, KJV).

Reflect on the passage above and answer the following questions:

When Solomon writes of vision, he is referring to the contact between God and the human spirit. He states there is no vision without direct connection or communication with God, and thus, no life. How do your relationship and daily communion with God inform your perspectives and aspirations?

_____
_____
_____
_____
_____
_____
_____

Has God given you a vision for your life? Why do you think it is so imperative to have vision? Are you adequately prioritizing your vision-casting?

_____
_____
_____
_____
_____
_____
_____

Small, seemingly insignificant habits and choices can derail the biggest and best of intentions. What are those little things in your life that interfere with your goals? Self-talk? Lack of self-control? Consider how these habits may be derailing you.

_____

_____

_____

_____

_____

RESPOND

Reaching your goals and fulfilling your purpose will not happen by chance. You have to plan each step along the way. Have you done so? Set aside time to chart your course from your current location to your aspirational destination.

_____
_____
_____
_____
_____
_____
_____
_____
_____

What's your endgame? How will you know when you've reached "there"?

_____
_____
_____
_____
_____
_____
_____
_____
_____

chapter 3

See 'N Say

If you're ready to change your life or move from "here" to "there," then there's no time like the present. It's time to open your eyes, look around, look up, look within, look everywhere until you lock eyes on your vision. Then, despite everything that may interfere with your line of sight, make a decision right here and right now to not look away.

REVIEW

Read Chapter 3: "See 'N Say" in Limitless: Defy the Ordinary, *reflect on the text, and answer the questions below.*

Mahalia Jackson's gentle nudge to Dr. Martin Luther King, Jr., led to one of history's most enduring moments. If someone encouraged you to "Tell them about the dream," what would you say?

_____
_____
_____
_____
_____
_____
_____
_____

Michael Jordan and Jack Nicklaus are known for visualizing their games and competitions. Why do you think this technique leads to success? Have you envisioned your destination?

_____
_____
_____
_____
_____
_____
_____
_____

What you see is what you'll say. What you say is what you'll get. Are you paying attention to the words you are speaking? Why does language have so much power over our motivations and actions?

_____
_____
_____
_____
_____
_____
_____

God was particular about when Joshua should speak and when he should not. How would you rate yourself on tact and restraint? Do you find it difficult to rein in your tongue? Why or why not?

_____
_____
_____
_____
_____
_____
_____

Who has spoken over your life in the past? If you have no one to speak encouragement or wisdom over you, are you prepared to speak affirmations over your own life?

_____
_____
_____
_____

When a couple gets married, their words bring them together in covenant before God. With whom or what are your words placing you in covenant right now?

REFLECT

"Remember not the former things, nor consider the things of old. Behold, I am doing a new thing; now it springs forth, do you not perceive it? I will make a way in the wilderness and rivers in the desert" (Isaiah 43:18-19, ESV).

Reflect on the passage above and answer the following questions:

God-sized dreams require God-sized vision. How does your vision align with His?

_____
_____
_____
_____
_____
_____
_____
_____

God's redeeming love erases the pain of our past when we allow it. What are you still holding on to that is inhibiting your journey towards a "new thing"?

_____
_____
_____
_____
_____
_____
_____
_____

What wilderness experiences has God led you through? Are you in the middle of one right now? Write down the different ways you have seen God in the most desolate of circumstances. Are you able to find confidence in His capacity to lead you today, given His previous faithfulness? Why or why not?

_____
_____
_____
_____
_____
_____
_____
_____
_____
_____
_____

RESPOND

Where do you want to be in five years? What do you wish for your children or community? Articulate and write down your aspirational five-year destination.

_____
_____
_____
_____
_____
_____
_____
_____

Negative self-talk is just as, if not more so, detrimental to your success and fulfillment as that which comes from others. Consider a recent conversation you had, a comment you made, or words you uttered to yourself in the mirror, and ask these questions about your statements:
- » Were my words true?
- » Were they helpful?
- » Were they inspiring?
- » Were they necessary?
- » Were they kind?

Write down your responses. Contemplate your answers and pray for God to reveal the truth about your words and intentions so that you may move closer to the limitless life He has designed for you.

_____
_____
_____

chapter 4

Flux Capacity

God didn't save you and me to sit week after week. His definition of faithful is not doing nothing. God saved you to take the gifts He's put inside of you and use them to minister to others. We were not saved to sit. We have been saved to get—get going, get moving—and do something.

REVIEW

Read Chapter 4: "Flux Capacity" in Limitless: Defy the Ordinary, *reflect on the text, and answer the questions below.*

Explain the concept of flux capacity in your own words. Can you identify the presence of flux capacity in your life? Where?

_____
_____
_____
_____
_____
_____
_____

How is your pyramid positioned? Are you standing at a broad base, looking upwards to a narrow future with few possibilities, or do you see your future as an expanse of possibility? Do you believe there are still dreams and goals you can accomplish, or is that phase of your life over?

_____
_____
_____
_____
_____
_____
_____
_____

The potential of your capacity directly correlates with your willingness to take action. If you are feeling stuck or feeling like your opportunities are few or limited in scope, can you draw any correlation between those feelings and your current mode of action? Are there things you are or are not doing that are limiting your capacity?

_____
_____
_____
_____
_____
_____
_____

Summarize the Dixie cup metaphor in your own words. Which container are you? To which do you aspire, and what is holding you back?

_____
_____
_____
_____
_____
_____
_____

Read aloud the quote from Pastor A. W. Tozer (page 77). What does it mean to you?

_____
_____
_____

_____

_____

_____

_____

E. L. Yates had no idea there was a fortune of resources and wealth just beneath the surface of his land. What is beneath your surface? Ask God today to reveal your hidden potential and implore him to help you identify it, understand it, and release it.

_____

_____

_____

_____

_____

_____

REFLECT

His master said to him, "Well done, good and faithful servant. You have been faithful over a little; I will set you over much. Enter into the joy of your master" (Matthew 25:2, ESV).

Reflect on the passage above and answer the following questions:

Consider the three men who received the talents. With which man do you most identify? Why? How do you feel about the similarities between him and you?

_____
_____
_____
_____
_____
_____
_____

Do you think the master's anger is justified? Why was the wasting of the talent such an offense? Are you wasting or hiding your own God-given talents? How do you think God perceives how you are or are not using what He has given you?

_____
_____
_____
_____
_____
_____
_____

There is a necessary element of risk in investments. The servant who received the most talents invested them with only hope—not a guarantee—of a good return. Some might call that faith. Do you have the faith to roll your dice and take a chance on a potentially worthwhile investment? Do you trust that God will provide what you need to see a return?

_____
_____
_____
_____
_____
_____
_____
_____

RESPOND

As a baby grows in the womb, the mother's internal organs shift to accommodate its increasing size. Are there things in your life that need to be moved around or eliminated to accommodate your growth? Write them down, and create a course of action to address each one.

_____
_____
_____
_____
_____
_____
_____
_____

Has a fear of failure manifested in your life? What has it prevented you from achieving? How has it impacted your willingness to take risks? Write down the three biggest fears holding you back. Trace their origins. One by one, consider the rationality of your fears, then determine what you need to dismantle them. Make a list of practical steps you must take to do so and follow through with intentionality.

_____
_____
_____
_____
_____
_____
_____
_____

chapter 5

Defining Moments

We cannot live our lives so focused on what is in front of us that we forget what is behind us. We can't allow the fear of today to negate the miracles of yesterday. At the same time, we can't get so consumed by the past or present that we forget the next mountaintop is within reach. We must live where celebration and anticipation coexist. This is where the promise of God dwells.

REVIEW

Read Chapter 5: "Defining Moments" in Limitless: Defy the Ordinary, *reflect on the text, and answer the questions below.*

Can you identify one or more defining moments in your life? What was their significance?

_____
_____
_____
_____
_____
_____
_____

When Petree received the news of his unborn child's potential diagnosis, his first instinct was to reach out to family, friends, and other church leaders. His second instinct was to hit his knees. When you receive life-altering news or encounter a potentially explosive scenario, whom do you turn to instinctively? If not God, why?

_____
_____
_____
_____
_____
_____
_____

What does it mean to live life between miracles? How do you see God in the valleys?

_____
_____
_____
_____
_____

Do you find yourself so distracted by the problems of today that you forget the miracles of yesterday? What has God brought you through in your life you can hold on to right now?

_____
_____
_____
_____
_____
_____
_____

On the other hand, are you so consumed by past or present struggles that you forget the next mountaintop is within reach? How can you remain aware of the promises of God that are still to come?

_____
_____
_____
_____
_____
_____
_____

REFLECT

"Have I not commanded you? Be strong and courageous. Do not be frightened, and do not be dismayed, for the Lord your God is with you wherever you go" (Joshua 1:9, ESV).

Reflect on the passage above and answer the following questions:

Joshua's momentous declaration to the leaders and other dignitaries at Shechem came toward the end of his life. Have you discounted your significance or impact due to your age? What can you take away from Joshua's story?

_____
_____
_____
_____
_____
_____
_____

When you encounter opposition, you can either quit or stand and fight. How might you muster the strength to take on challenges? Do you believe God will fortify you?

_____
_____
_____
_____
_____
_____

RESPOND

"As for me and my house, we will serve the Lord," (Joshua 24:15, NIV) is one of the most well-known verses in Scripture. What do those words mean to you and your family? How can you put the act of serving God into action within your household?

_____
_____
_____
_____
_____
_____
_____
_____
_____

The moment can define you, or you can define the moment. If you face the impossible, have you taken the time to reflect on how God has carried you through dark waters before? Are you ready to choose right here, right now, whom you will serve?

_____
_____
_____
_____
_____
_____
_____
_____
_____
_____
_____
_____

chapter 6

Within Reach

Not everyone becomes who God has intended them to become because few people are ready to dig in and do the hard work that change requires. But, if you are to live fully in the role to which He has called you, prepare yourself for leaving what is familiar and venturing into the unknown.

REVIEW

Read Chapter 6: "Within Reach" in Limitless: Defy the Ordinary, *reflect on the text, and answer the questions below.*

How were the different 40-year periods that comprised Moses' life characterized? Do you identify with any of his experiences in your own life or times of transition?

_____
_____
_____
_____
_____
_____
_____
_____
_____

Why do you think it would be difficult—even impossible—to know who you are if you don't know who God is?

_____
_____
_____
_____
_____
_____
_____
_____
_____

Have you ever felt as though you were treading water? Have you felt like the activities or work in which you are engaged are meaningless? How can you step into faith and believe that nothing, even those things which feel pointless, is wasted?

_____
_____
_____
_____
_____
_____
_____

Has God called you to a task or a mission for which you felt unprepared? How did you respond?

_____
_____
_____
_____
_____
_____
_____

When God charged Moses with leading His people to freedom, Moses questioned his adequacy. He had once been a prince but was now a shepherd. He had been a murderer and was told to become a deliverer. His identity was a source of uncertainty. Is yours? Do you know who you are? How can you feel secure in your capacity to fulfill your calling?

_____
_____
_____
_____

How do you handle control or the lack of it? How has your perception and practice of management impacted your success?

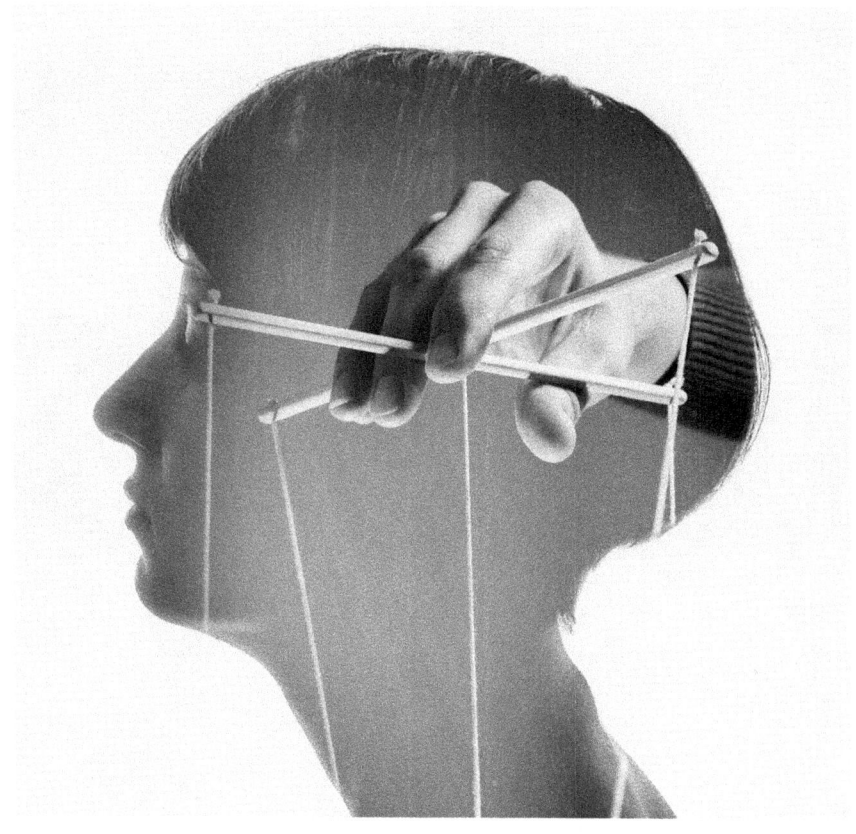

After fulfilling his call and wandering through the desert for 40 years, Moses had a momentary loss of control and disobedience that robbed him of entrance to the Promised Land. Can you recall when you experienced something similar? How did that impact you? What can you learn from that experience?

_____
_____
_____
_____
_____
_____
_____
_____
_____

REFLECT

Then Moses said to God, "If I come to the people of Israel and say to them, 'The God of your fathers has sent me to you,' and they ask me, 'What is his name?' what shall I say to them?" God said to Moses, "I AM who I AM." And he said, "Say this to the people of Israel: 'I AM has sent me to you'" (Exodus 3:13-14, ESV).

Reflect on the passage above and answer the following questions:

From where do you suppose Moses' trepidation arose? Why was it necessary to know the name of the One by whom he had been sent?

_____
_____
_____
_____
_____
_____
_____
_____

God is known by many names. Read through the various forms of His names on page 98. Do you recognize these characteristics? Reflect on the ways these manifestations of God have impacted you.

_____
_____
_____
_____
_____

_____

_____

_____

Can you recall a time in your life when God has explicitly sent you somewhere to do something, and you said no? Or perhaps a time when you said yes? Reflect on the emotions and considerations you wrestled with as you attempted to meet or walk away from God's will. What impact did that decision have on your relationship with Him?

_____

_____

_____

_____

_____

_____

_____

RESPOND

Even after God demonstrated His power to Moses and helped him understand who he was in light of who God is, Moses continued to grasp for excuses to avoid this mission. Have you ever given excuses to others, God, or even yourself to get out of a calling? Is this habitual? If so, examine what may be at the core of your reluctance.

_____
_____
_____
_____
_____
_____
_____
_____

Do the opinions of others weigh on you? Have you ever backed away from a calling or purpose for fear of what others might think? If so, why do you think that is? What are ways you can shift your attention away from what others may be thinking about you to what God knows about you?

_____
_____
_____
_____
_____
_____
_____
_____

chapter 7

Tuned by Tension

While we endure hardship, we remain tethered to God's unconditional love. It's much easier to see and feel that love at certain times in life than in seasons of pain. Regardless of our capacity or willingness to accept His love, it never moves or changes.

REVIEW

Read Chapter 7: "Tuned by Tension" in Limitless: Defy the Ordinary, *reflect on the text, and answer the questions below.*

Petree describes the loss of his sister as "searing," the pain exacerbated due to the sudden, traumatic nature of her death. Can you relate to his experience? Take time to write down your trauma and its lasting impact on you.

_____
_____
_____
_____
_____
_____
_____
_____

When Paul states that all things will eventually turn out well for those who love the Lord, he acknowledges things aren't necessarily good yet; there is a dichotomy between the present struggle and future hope. How have you experienced this?

_____
_____
_____
_____
_____
_____
_____
_____

Have you ever tuned a guitar? If so, what are your recollections about the relationship and necessity of tension relative to pitch and tone? How do these same elements—tension, pitch, and tone—manifest in your life?

_____
_____
_____
_____
_____
_____

In your words, explain the difference between tension and stress. Identify areas of your life that are ruled by one or the other or both.

_____
_____
_____
_____
_____
_____

B. F. Skinner used a button to condition pigeons. The "Like" button tends to have a similar effect on humans, often with detrimental repercussions. How aware are you of the likes/dislikes/comments from others regarding you? How do they affect you daily?

_____
_____
_____
_____
_____
_____

REFLECT

And we know that for those who love God all things work together for good, for those who are called according to his purpose (Romans 8:28, ESV).

Reflect on the passage above and answer the following questions:

If you or others you know have experienced tragedy, have you wondered how a "good" God could allow such things? How do you reconcile that, or have you been able to do so?

_____
_____
_____
_____
_____
_____
_____
_____

God designed us to live within the tension of heaven and earth, using our challenges to tune and refine us. Do you feel capable of resting in the middle of that tension? Why or why not?

_____
_____
_____
_____
_____
_____
_____
_____

Do you have difficulty accepting the support of others in difficult times? Are you able to allow God to use others to care for you in your struggles? Why might this be important?

_____
_____
_____
_____
_____
_____
_____
_____

RESPOND

Paul addressed his personal struggles and habits that interfered with the life he wanted to lead. What habits do you have that are hindering your goals or personal development? Identify them, and consider strategies you can implement to overcome them.

_____
_____
_____
_____
_____
_____
_____
_____

Fear of Missing Out (FOMO) is an authentic condition that can wreak havoc in your life. Have you experienced FOMO? Do you notice a correlation between social media habits (if you engage in social media) and this feeling? Consider how altering your social media usage might benefit you. What are practical steps to improve the time you spend online?

_____
_____
_____
_____
_____
_____
_____
_____
_____

Consider the various tragedies and trials you have experienced and survived. How have these shaped the person you are today? How can you use those experiences to fortify you when new challenges arise?

_____
_____
_____
_____
_____
_____
_____
_____
_____

chapter 8

A Room With a View

When I start to lose my view, when things get distorted, and I can no longer visualize what's ahead of me, I have to remember that the solution will not be about what I can do or how good I am. I am nothing but an earthen vessel. What's valuable is the treasure on the inside—God's power, not mine.

REVIEW

Read Chapter 8: "A Room with A View" in Limitless: Defy the Ordinary, *reflect on the text, and answer the questions below.*

Consider the story of the two men in the hospital, as told on pages 121-123. With which of these two men do you more closely identify? Explain your answer.

_____
_____
_____
_____
_____
_____
_____
_____

Can you recall a time when you took in a beautiful view? The top of a hotel? The Grand Canyon? A mountaintop? What struck you about the landscape or cityscape? Why do you think sensory experiences like that stay with us?

_____
_____
_____
_____
_____
_____
_____
_____

Bitterness blocks; forgiveness flows. If you choose to be bitter, you will block every blessing of God from coming into your life. Choose to get better; refuse to get bitter. What grudge are you holding onto that is blocking your view?

_____
_____
_____
_____
_____
_____
_____

What is the importance of having a clear vision for your life? Do you have one? If so, write it down. If not, what's standing in your way of developing or harnessing a vision?

_____
_____
_____
_____
_____
_____
_____

If the opposite of faith is certainty, what role does fear play? Can faith and fear coexist?

_____
_____
_____
_____

Social media has nurtured a culture of reaction, diminishing the prevalence of introspection. What are your observations about your own behavior online? Are you more prone to reacting without thinking? What repercussions have you experienced from this type of behavior?

REFLECT

Whatever is true, whatever is honorable, whatever is just, whatever is pure, whatever is lovely, whatever is commendable, if there is any excellence, if there is anything worthy of praise, think about these things (Philippians 4:8, ESV).

Reflect on the passage above and answer the following questions:

Why is it important to keep our minds on things that are good and excellent? What is the impact of our thoughts upon the rest of our lives?

_____
_____
_____
_____
_____
_____
_____
_____

How do you determine what is good? How do you know what is pure? Knowing that God is the epitome of goodness, how might an intimate knowledge of His nature enhance your capacity to discern between good, evil, honorable, and dishonorable?

_____
_____
_____
_____

_____

_____

_____

_____

Do you believe God created you for possibilities? Do you believe He instilled within you the seeds of greatness? If so, how might your thoughts be the food that nurtures what He has already begun?

_____

_____

_____

_____

_____

_____

_____

_____

RESPOND

Between demands at home, school, work, or other obligations, our finite energy stores are being tapped from multiple sources. Given that this can lead to burnout, fatigue, and diminished performance, how can you streamline your daily outputs, so you are putting your energy into those things which produce the most good?

_____

_____

_____

_____

_____

_____

_____

Life has no shortage of drama. Often, we tend to seek it out, latching onto the latest tragedy, indignity, or problem. While it's essential and a good thing to be informed about the world around us, it's all too easy to spend the bulk of our time and energy looking for problems. Bitterness comes more easily than wisdom and deference. If you find yourself perpetually on the hunt for the issues, what can you do to change this?

_____

_____

_____

_____

_____

_____

_____

chapter 9

A Blessing Called Rejection

There is a purpose behind your rejection. You may not see it right now, and it can be excruciating, but God has placed you where you are for a purpose.

REVIEW

Read Chapter 9: "A Blessing Called Rejection" in Limitless: Defy the Ordinary, reflect on the text, and answer the questions below.

Walt Disney was unbelievably mischaracterized when he lost a job early in his career. What impact do you think that experience may have had upon him? Is it possible his dismissal was a good thing?

_____
_____
_____
_____
_____
_____
_____
_____

Describe a time when you experienced rejection. How did it impact your psyche? Did it deter you from or spur you toward action?

_____
_____
_____
_____
_____
_____
_____
_____

Conditional rejection is based on performance. How have you experienced this? Have you treated others with disregard due to performance issues? How do you think God perceives you and your shortcomings?

___

Emotional rejection is often as hard to receive as it is to avoid. How have you allowed your heart or emotions to dictate your interaction with others? If this is a particularly debilitating area, what are three things you can do to combat the control your emotions have over you?

___

Celebrity rejection may seem irrelevant to you. However, it is symptomatic of a culture that erects and tears down others with ease. What does this phenomenon mean to you? Do you experience repercussions from this cultural paradigm?

_____
_____
_____
_____
_____
_____
_____
_____
_____
_____

Irrational rejection is perhaps the most injurious form of rejection. Because there is no logic, the dismissal can't be explained or reconciled, potentially wreaking havoc on the recipient's self-worth. Have you been on the receiving end of such rejection? How did you cope?

_____

_____

_____

_____

_____

_____

_____

_____

_____

_____

REFLECT

"The stone that the builders rejected has become the cornerstone; this was the Lord's doing, and it is marvelous in our eyes ..." (Matthew 21:42, ESV)

Reflect on the passage above and answer the following questions:

Have you ever considered the rejection Jesus experienced throughout His life? How does it make you feel knowing He understands the pain of rejection? Does it change the way you perceive the dismissals or rejection you have experienced?

_____
_____
_____
_____
_____
_____

Jesus' humility, compassion, and unconditional love were on full display when He washed the feet of His two would-be betrayers. How do you engage with those who have treated you poorly? What can you learn from Jesus' generosity of spirit?

_____
_____
_____
_____
_____
_____

When you know God's acceptance, you can endure man's rejection. What rejection are you still holding onto that God has intended for your healing?

_____
_____
_____
_____
_____
_____
_____

RESPOND

What is the correlation between rejection and physical pain? Is this surprising to you? Identify two coping habits—one negative and one positive—in which you have engaged to alleviate the visceral impact of rejection.

_____
_____
_____
_____
_____
_____
_____
_____
_____

Self-rejection can be debilitating and difficult to overcome. Can you trace a pattern of rejection from others over your lifetime that has led to a rejection of self? How can you use that information to improve your outlook on your life and limitations?

_____
_____
_____
_____
_____
_____
_____
_____

chapter 10

The Seventh Wave

Surviving is what you can do. Thriving is what you need God to do. Surviving is playing it safe. Thriving is taking risks of faith and deciding not to fear what God can use to help you grow.

REVIEW

Read Chapter 10: "The Seventh Wave" in Limitless: Defy the Ordinary, reflect on the text, and answer the questions below.

Imagine you are on the boat on the Sea of Galilee. The storm is raging, Jesus is walking toward you, and Peter's about to jump out. What's going through your mind? Are you closing your eyes, hoping it will be over soon? Grabbing a life preserver for your soon-to-be-fallen friend? Ready to join Peter in the maelstrom? Consider your reaction below.

_____
_____
_____
_____
_____
_____
_____
_____

Did you recall Jesus' walk on waves immediately followed the feeding of the 5,000? The disciples witnessed these events back-to-back, yet they remained in disbelief as their Savior approached. Think of a time when the waves of life threatened to consume you. Did your faith in your miracle-working Creator sustain you? What instances can you reference in your life that reveal the wonders of God?

_____
_____
_____
_____
_____
_____
_____
_____

There are two different types of people—those who see the waves and run for safety, and those who see the waves and run straight for them, lost in the exhilaration of the moment. To which group do you belong? Why?

___
___
___
___
___
___
___
___

Bethany Hamilton is the embodiment of the seventh-wave surfer. Nothing could pull her from the waves—not even a shark. What characteristics does she possess that you admire? Do you see any of those within yourself?

_____

_____

_____

_____

_____

_____

_____

_____

_____

REFLECT

"Lord, if it's you," Peter replied, "tell me to come to you on the water." "Come," he said (Matthew 14:29, NIV).

Reflect on the passage above and answer the following questions:

The story of Jesus and Peter walking on water is one of the most iconic stories in history. What does it mean to you?

_____

_____

_____

_____

When Peter began to slip below the water, Jesus asked him why he doubted. Why do you doubt? To whom do you reach when you start to fall?

_____

_____

_____

_____

Waves don't hide Jesus; they reveal Him. What waves are you hiding from today? Do you see Jesus in them? Can you hear His voice?

_____

_____

_____

_____

RESPOND

Recent events have been relentless—storms seemingly pounding the entire globe without discrimination or mercy. Did you survive? Did you thrive? What are two positive things that came out of your time in quarantine or other crisis?

_____
_____
_____
_____
_____
_____
_____
_____
_____

How will you make the most of your next wave? What can you do now to be able to ride out the rising, relentless waters of life?

_____
_____
_____
_____
_____
_____
_____
_____
_____
_____

chapter 11

That's Life

You can't predict the cards you'll draw or craft the circumstances of your life and the people in it. You have as much control over most people and places in your life as you do, controlling whether the sky will be filled with sunshine or rain clouds. But you do have a choice. You always have a choice, and your life will eventually become a collective of those choices.

REVIEW

Read Chapter 11: "That's Life" in Limitless: Defy the Ordinary, *reflect on the text, and answer the questions below.*

Can you identify with Michelle's story? Have you experienced something traumatic? Did you translate your suffering as a failure?

___

You have little to no control as to the cards you will be dealt in life. Does this lack of control instill fear or bitterness in you? Is it hard to trust in God's goodness when the cards are stacked against you?

___

The story of Hagar is full of broken people, misplaced trust, emotionally-charged actions … you know—life. Sarah felt dejected because she could not have children. She sensed the judgment of the community around her and grew impatient for God to pull through on His promise to make her a mother. Overwhelmed, she made a rash decision that led to centuries of repercussions, not to mention permanently altering the state of her marriage. Can you understand her desperation? What would you have done in those circumstances?

_____
_____
_____
_____
_____
_____
_____
_____

Hagar did not choose to carry Abraham's child; she was ordered to. What are you carrying around that was never your choice in the first place? What is your "Hagar" moment, and how does it impact you today?

_____
_____
_____
_____
_____
_____
_____
_____

When Hagar, the victim, began to develop her baby bump, she lorded it over Sarah, who treated her harshly. Things escalated, and Hagar eventually had enough and left. Have you ever allowed pride to get the best of you? What was the outcome?

Why do you think God sent Hagar back to a place of pain? What does the concept of submission mean to you, and is it something you are capable of and willing to do?

REFLECT

"In the world you will have tribulation. But take heart; I have overcome the world" (John 16:33b, ESV).

Reflect on the passage above and answer the following questions:

How do you interpret this verse? Is this a truth you know only in your head, or does your heart truly believe God has you no matter what?

_____
_____
_____
_____
_____
_____
_____
_____

Control is a slippery slope coming and going. We spend most of our lives trying to control the things around us—relationships, work, politics, and the list goes on. Why? To avoid pain. What is your relationship to control? Has this been a positive or negative force in your life? How does your understanding of God's redeeming love impact your experience of pain and the need to control it?

_____

_____

_____

_____

_____

_____

_____

_____

_____

RESPOND

Think about the two frogs. Each encountered a situation beyond its control. One gave up, and the other chose to fight. That frog even decided to believe that the naysayers were on his side. Which frog are you? Why?

_____
_____
_____
_____
_____
_____
_____
_____
_____

The promise is always bigger than the pain. What choices can you make today to loosen your grip on the pain and move closer to the promise of God's blessings? Are you ready to believe that the life He has for you is more significant than the pain of today?

_____
_____
_____
_____
_____
_____
_____
_____
_____

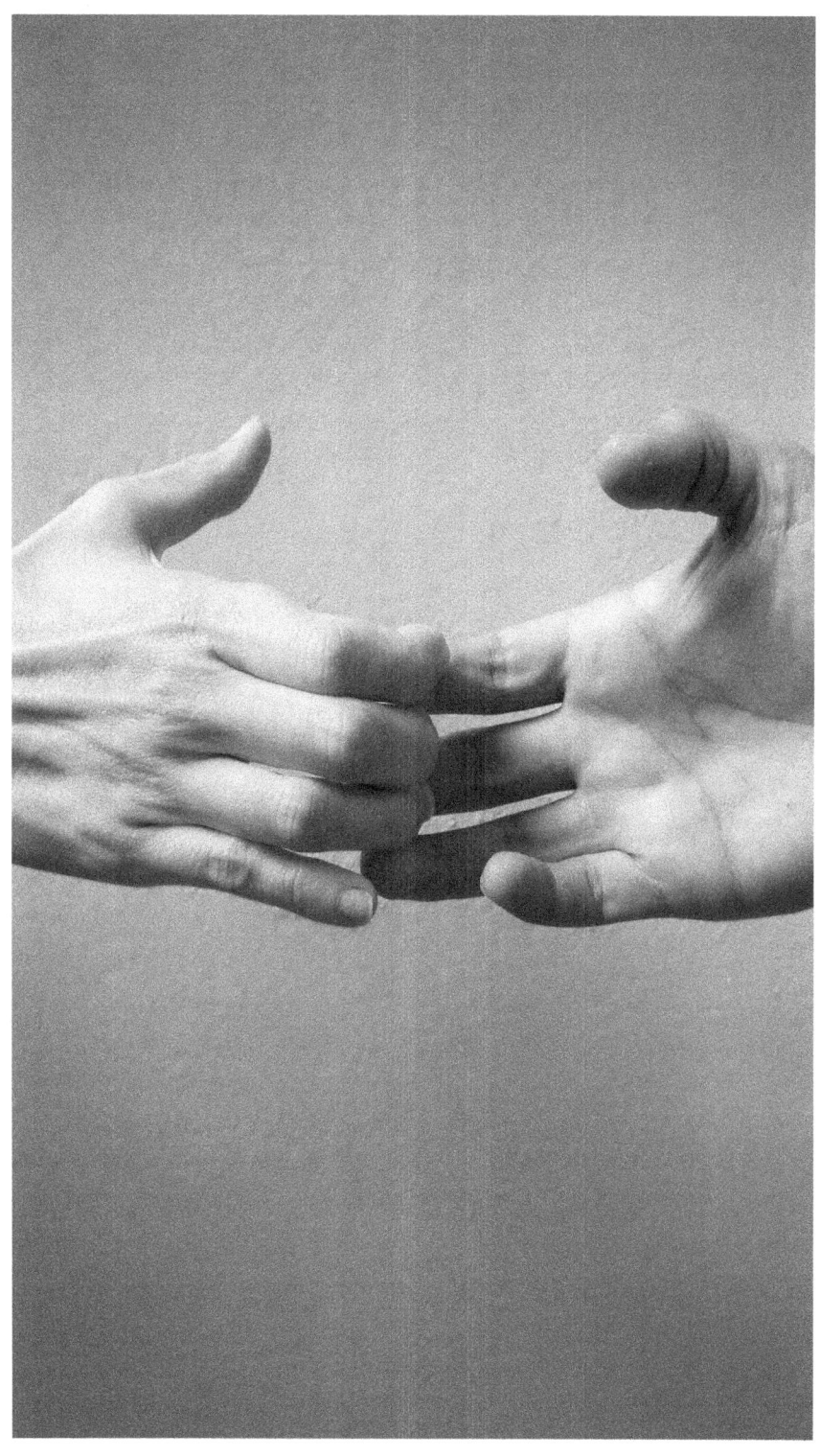

chapter 12

Finding Your Greatness

As a child of the Living God, you have everything you need to be great. You lack nothing. The challenge will be to abandon your excuses, ignore the judgment of the world, and live into your purpose. Take Jesus with you on your journey to greatness, and don't ever look back.

REVIEW

Read Chapter 12: "Finding Your Greatness" in Limitless: Defy the Ordinary, *reflect on the text, and answer the questions below.*

The two little girls born into hardship had every reason to fail. What circumstances did you inherit, and how have they impacted the way you live your life?

_____
_____
_____
_____
_____
_____
_____
_____
_____

Do you believe you have the seeds of greatness within you? If not, why? If so, what have you done with them?

_____
_____
_____
_____
_____
_____
_____
_____
_____

The Olympics Nike ads celebrated a type of greatness typically overlooked in our celebrity-infused society. Rather than focus on the well-known athletes and champions, they featured everyday kids, men, and women displaying greatness. The underlying message: Greatness can come from anywhere. Where have you discovered greatness you weren't expecting?

_____

_____

_____

_____

_____

_____

_____

_____

Can you identify with the fear Petree experienced during his rappelling adventure? How does this story embody the concept that "greatness is scary until it isn't"? Have you experienced anything similar? What did you learn from your situation?

_____

_____

_____

_____

_____

_____

_____

_____

Review the Allyson Felix and Kerri Strugg stories (pp. 186-188). How do their victories strike you? Do you find it encouraging that greatness doesn't hinge on aesthetics? Has this notion played out in your life? Ponder a time when you sacrificed looks for the win. Are you prepared to do so again?

_____
_____
_____
_____
_____
_____
_____
_____
_____

Social media has turned daily life into a trial by jury, of sorts. Everyone seemingly has an opinion on everyone else. Tact is a long-lost art form, sacrificed for the sake of a tweet or a post created to put someone down. How big of a role does the judgment of others play in your life?

_____
_____
_____
_____
_____
_____
_____
_____
_____

Do you allow it to bring you down? Have you passed judgment on others? How have your words impacted them?

_____
_____
_____
_____
_____
_____
_____
_____
_____

Consider the meteoric rise of Simone Biles and the full life Ellie has lived. What makes their success so special? What inspiration can you find in their stories?

_____
_____
_____
_____
_____
_____
_____
_____
_____
_____
_____
_____

REFLECT

"Choose this day, whom you will serve" (Joshua 24:15, ESV).

Reflect on the passage above and answer the following questions:

There is no halfway when it comes to living into your greatness. You have to choose to be all in. Whom have you chosen to serve today?

_____
_____
_____
_____
_____
_____
_____

Esther was not born to be great, yet she ascended to the throne and fulfilled a historic mission. She chose to rise above her station and serve God faithfully, even at great risk. Think about your origin story. Do you allow your beginnings to hinder your capacity? Or have you decided to rise above your circumstances?

_____

_____

_____

_____

_____

_____

_____

_____

_____

King David and Michael Phelps share something in common. While others didn't know who they were or what they could do, they chose to trust their God-given abilities. Their confidence and commitment to cultivating their talents and wisdom enabled them to soar. Do you believe in your greatness? Are you ready to invest in yourself to achieve the limitless life for which you were created?

_____

_____

_____

_____

_____

_____

_____

_____

_____

RESPOND

Discuss the differences between talent and teachability. Do you consider yourself a teachable person? What are some of the personal characteristics you should pursue to become humble and teachable?

_____
_____
_____
_____
_____
_____
_____
_____

What is holding you back from embracing all that God has placed within you? Are you waiting for the affirmation of others? How much longer are you planning to wait? What will it take for you to leap into the life God desires for you? Write down five goals to complete in the coming year to bring you closer to your greatness and the fulfillment of your call.

_____
_____
_____
_____
_____
_____
_____
_____
_____
_____

Defy the Ordinary

www.ingramcontent.com/pod-product-compliance
Lightning Source LLC
Chambersburg PA
CBHW070204100426
42743CB00013B/3037